C000185295

Series consultant: Dr Dorothy Rowe

The author and publisher would like to thank the
staff and pupils of the Charles Dickens J & I School,
London; the East Leeds Family Learning Centre, Leeds;
Mayfield Primary School, Cambridge and Swavesey Village
College, Cambridge for their help in making this book.

A CIP catalogue record for this book
is available from the British Library.

ISBN 0-7136-5051-6

Printed by A & C Black (Publishers) Limited
35 Bedford Row, London WC1R 4JH

Text copyright
© 1999 Althea Braithwaite
Photographs copyright
© 1999 Charlie Best
Illustrations copyright
© 1999 Conny Jude

All rights reserved. No part of this publication may be
reproduced or used in any form or by any means –
photographic, electronic or mechanical, including
photocopying, recording, taping or information storage
and retrieval systems – without the prior written
permission of the publishers.

Typeset in 15/19 pt Sabon Roman and
13/19 pt Futura Bold Oblique.

Printed in Hong Kong through Colorcraft Ltd.

CHOICES

Feeling Sad

Althea

Photographs by
Charlie Best

Illustrations by
Conny Jude

A & C Black
London

Everyone feels sad at times. Even little things can make us unhappy.

Here are some of the things that make us sad.

When it's raining and I can't go out to play.

Having a row with a friend.

When I broke my favourite mug.

When my hamster died.

When I get left out.

Sometimes when I feel unhappy, I don't even know the reason why.

When my mum cries it makes me feel sad. I think it must be something I have done.

What makes you sad?

3

How do you feel when you are sad?

I feel ill and my throat swells up.

When I'm sad I feel really cold inside. It's a sort of empty feeling.

I feel heavy.

I get a lump in my throat and I cry for no reason.

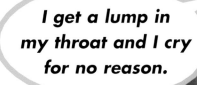

Sadness and anger often go together.

Joe says that when his new bike was stolen, he felt very angry and very sad at the same time.

> When I'm sad I don't know what to do with myself, so I get angry. When I upset paint all over my new shoes I took it out on my friend. Later I told her I was sorry.

When you have been feeling miserable it's a good idea to try to do things to cheer yourself up. Polly says that if she can make herself join in a game with her friends, she finds that after a while she realises she's not feeling sad any more.

Sue says that just going out into the garden to see the flowers and listen to birds singing makes her feel better.

I kick a football as hard as I can.

Sometimes I burst into tears, then I feel better.

Amit says he wants to be on his own. "I hate crying in front of people. I shut myself away." He says it doesn't help when other people tell him to cheer up. "It makes me think that I should be feeling happy and that makes me feel even worse."

Even when you're told to be cheerful, don't tell yourself you're happy when you're not, because then you'll go on feeling sad inside. You need to understand why you are feeling sad before you can feel better. It helps to talk about your feelings. Who do you talk to when you are feeling sad?

> *I was really upset when my best friend moved to another country.*

Some things that make us sad go on happening and we have to learn to live with them. It helps if you have someone you can talk to about how you're feeling.

Don said he felt really sad and scared when his mum had to go into hospital. "She was in there for months." What made it worse for Don was that he didn't know what was happening. "Dad couldn't really talk about it."

Sometimes a parent has to work away from home. The family all miss each other and look forward to when they can be together again.

"When Daddy is away, I feel unhappy and lonely. It's great when he phones and we all get a chance to talk to him. Mum is helping me keep a diary of the things we are doing, to show Dad when he comes home."

My dad doesn't live with us any more. That makes me very sad.

Sometimes parents break up and one of them leaves home for good. It's because they decide they can't live together any more. Children sometimes think that it must be something they have done. That's never the reason. You must not start blaming yourself.

All families have to cope with a major sadness from time to time.

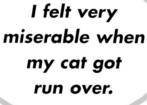

Our dog got ill and we had to have him put down. We all cried when we buried him in the garden.

I felt very miserable when my cat got run over.

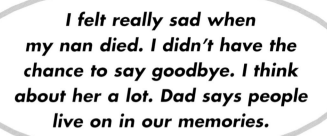

I felt really sad when my nan died. I didn't have the chance to say goodbye. I think about her a lot. Dad says people live on in our memories.

I badly miss my uncle. He wasn't old when he died.

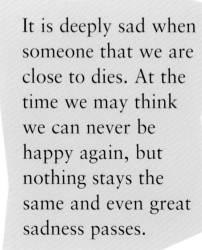

It is deeply sad when someone that we are close to dies. At the time we may think we can never be happy again, but nothing stays the same and even great sadness passes.

Great sadness is difficult to describe.
Sometimes, it can be a physical feeling.

Sometimes sadness can make us feel
confused, as if we're breaking up
and falling apart.

*It gave me an
awful pain in
my chest.*

Feeling sad can affect
the way we behave
towards others.

David says that when
he felt sad, he couldn't
concentrate on his
school work so he
played the fool. "I
wanted people to care
and take notice of me.
Instead they got angry."

How do we learn to cope with the terrible feeling of sadness we have when someone dies or leaves us?

It helps if the people involved talk to each other and share their feelings. Experiencing sadness helps us to understand and help other people when they are unhappy.

"Grandad was Mum's dad. When he died, we both felt very sad. Mum and I talked about the good times we had when we used to visit Grandad. We laugh together as we remember his jokes."

When you've lost something or someone that's very important to you, it's right to feel sad. But if you blame yourself for the disaster your sadness can turn into depression.

"When I was new at school, I used to get depressed when people said nasty things about me. I believed them. Now I have some friends, so I know I can't be all bad. I can see that those people were bullies."

Sometimes people get so depressed that they need help from someone outside the family.

"When my uncle died, I heard my aunt saying that life wasn't worth living. The doctor arranged for her to talk to a counsellor. She still misses my uncle, but she's all right again now."

My dad used to say that I was so noisy I gave him a headache. When he died I thought it was my fault. I felt there was an invisible wall all around me and I was on my own. It was terrible.

When people start blaming themselves for everything that goes wrong, they become depressed. If you start thinking you are a bad person then everything you do will seem bad to you. Instead, think of yourself as a good person who gets it wrong sometimes.

Jane found that she spent a lot of time with her friend, just listening when she talked.

"When Dad was depressed when he lost his job he didn't want to do anything or talk to anyone, so I'd sit with him in the living room while I did my homework. When he got better he told me that I'd comforted him a lot."

Sarah said that she was patient when her friend Jay started making a nuisance of himself. "He kept scooping up the marbles and messing up the game. Mum told me it was because his grandma had died. I tried not to get annoyed, but it was difficult."

It can be very annoying when friends start acting silly. If you can be patient with them and still let them join in your games, it will help a lot. They will know that you still care about them.

Marie remembers telling her friend silly jokes to try to cheer him up. "It made him laugh, then cry again."

"I know he's feeling sad, but at least he knows that I care about how he's feeling."

Becky's gran says she helped her by giving her lots of hugs when her grandad died.

"I think it helped both of us."

19

What is happiness? Everyone wants to feel that they are loved and cared for, and that someone needs them. What makes you feel happy?

When I am playing with my friends.

I do wheelies on my bike.

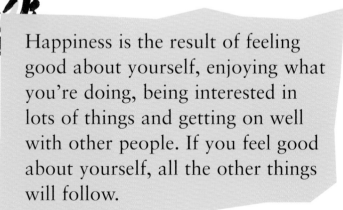

Happiness is the result of feeling good about yourself, enjoying what you're doing, being interested in lots of things and getting on well with other people. If you feel good about yourself, all the other things will follow.

When you're happy, how does it make you feel?

Feeling like the best!

When we are really happy my friend and I want to laugh and laugh and never stop. We keep saying silly things to keep laughing.

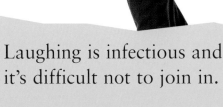

Laughing is infectious and it's difficult not to join in.

There is no other feeling like happiness. Sometimes it's mixed with excitement. You can't be excited without feeling happy!

If you smile at people, they often smile back. When you feel good about yourself your happiness can spread to other people.

Sadness is a natural part of life. Because we care about certain people and certain things, we feel sad if we lose them. If you think about it, the only way never to feel sad would be never to become attached to anybody or anything. But that would be a terrible way to live, far worse than being sad.

Good things can come out of feeling sad. Shared sadness can bring people together and make them feel closer to one another.

James says that because he has known what it's like to feel sad, he can enjoy the times when he feels happy all the more.

If you were never sad you wouldn't know when you were happy.

Sometimes we feel happy and sometimes we feel sad – both feelings are natural parts of life. If you're sad, remember the feeling of sadness won't go on forever. You can't store up happiness to use when you're feeling sad, so just enjoy the feeling of being happy.

23

For teachers and parents

A note from Dorothy Rowe

Parents and teachers want children to be happy, so when a child is sad parents and teachers have a problem. Telling the child to be happy or that there's nothing to be sad about only makes things harder for the child.
It's essential to accept that the child is sad and then to try to find out how the child sees the situation. What determines a person's behaviour is not what happens to that person but how that person interprets what has happened.

No two people see anything in exactly the same way, and a child never sees anything in the way an adult does. The child may give what seems to be a trivial reason for feeling sad, like losing a toy, but if the adult asks, 'Why was that toy important to you?' the child is likely to indicate that the toy represented something very important. The child may be sad about something which also causes the adult pain and, even though it can be hard for the adult to reveal a little of that pain, doing so helps the child understand that sadness is universal.

Feeling sad isn't a problem we can solve once and for all, but something we have to live with all our lives. The parent or teacher can help a child by talking about their own difficulties in dealing with sadness, while pointing out that sadness can bring people together in a way that not even happiness can do.

When going through the book again, it may be useful to consider some of the following points.

People can sometimes almost enjoy feeling sad; they cry when they watch a sad film on the TV, or when they read a sad book. It may bring back events in their lives when they were sad or it may be just that they are enjoying the emotion. They are not sad for themselves, but for the characters involved.

Page 3
Children need reassurance that, usually, they are not the cause of a parent's sadness.

Page 5
When someone is sad they sometimes turn a small argument with someone into something big, so they can become emotional.

Page 7
Children should know it's not babyish to cry when you feel sad. It sometimes helps to get it out, rather than let the emotion build up inside.

Sometimes children are not sure whether it's all right to feel better. They want to start playing again, but they feel they should still be feeling sad.

24

Page 10-11
Even when people are living with a sadness they feel happy for parts of the time. It's all right to laugh and feel happy too.

Page 13
Children can be very confused when adults try to hide their feeling of sadness. They need to know that their parents feel very unhappy too.

Adults sometimes don't realise that children are grieving, because in between feeling sad they spend a lot of their time laughing and playing together. Children should have it confirmed that it's good for them to do this.

Page 15
Adults need to recognise that children can become very depressed and even suicidal. Childline and The Samaritans receive phone calls from very young children seeking their help. When children are depressed they don't necessarily sit around and mope. Instead they may become very noisy and emotional, because they can't cope with the pain.

Page 16
When people are sad they may need to talk about the cause at great length, and they should be encouraged to do so.

Pages 20-21
If you know what makes you happy, you may be able to have a more positive approach to life and avoid some feelings of unhappiness. Get everyone to make a list of all the things that make them happy, and compare and talk about the results.

Further reading

Children may find it interesting and helpful to have a look at some of the following books which also deal with the subject of feeling sad.

Janine Amos
Sad
(Cherrytree, 1997)

Bernard Ashley
The Trouble with Donovan Croft
(Puffin, 1977)

Elizabeth Laird
Secret Friends
(Hodder Children's Books, 1996)

Jacqueline Wilson
Cliffhanger
(Corgi Yearling Books, 1995)